BEDFORD TO
WELLINGBOROUGH

Including Hitchin, Northampton and Higham Ferrers

Geoff Goslin
Series editor Vic Mitchell

MP Middleton Press

Cover picture: Ex-LNWR 2-4-0 no. 5031 Hardwicke *waits to depart for Wellingborough from the ex-MR terminus at Northampton St.John's Street sometime in 1931. Built at Crewe in 1892, the locomotive is now in the National Railway Museum. (L.Hanson)*

Published June 2004

ISBN 1 904474 31 4

© *Middleton Press, 2004*

Design   *David Pede*
Typesetting   *Barbara Mitchell*

Published by
           Middleton Press
           Easebourne Lane
           Midhurst, West Sussex
           GU29 9AZ
Tel: 01730 813169
Fax: 01730 812601
Email: info@middletonpress.co.uk
www.middletonpress.co.uk

Printed & bound by MPG Books Ltd, Bodmin, Cornwall

CONTENTS

INDEX

ACKNOWLEDGEMENTS

Reference has been made to notes compiled by the late Geoffrey Webb which have proved of great help. I am indebted to John Osgood and Peter Holmes for information. Thanks are due to Ken Fairey, who looked out and printed many of his photographs specially, and to all the other photographers whose work appears in this volume.

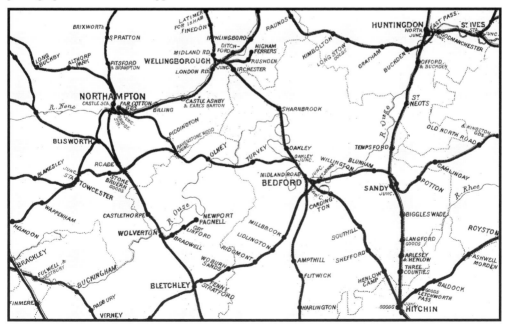

Railway Clearing House map of 1947.

GEOGRAPHICAL SETTING

The route from Hitchin to Bedford crosses several small watercourses and a variety of geological structures. It begins on the Chalk of the northern extension of the Chiltern Hills and drops onto the parallel Upper Greensand and Gault Clay outcrops. There follows narrow banks of Lower Greensand and Corallian Limestone, the latter necessitating a tunnel. About five miles of track runs over Oxford Clay before the line passes over the River Ouse at the county town of Bedford. This old market centre is situated on a small raised area of Limestone.

The main line follows the meandering River Ouse from Bedford to Sharnbrook, where a steep climb begins. The line passes over a ridge of Limestone, before descending equally steeply into the Nene Valley, at Wellingborough.

The branch to Northampton is mostly on Limestone. It drops down into the Ouse Valley at Olney and ends close to the River Nene at the county town, once well known for shoe making. The line at Olney is in Buckinghamshire and at Hitchin it is in Hertfordshire. The remainder of the routes are in Bedfordshire or Northamptonshire.

The maps are to the scale of 25ins to 1 mile with north at the top, unless otherwise indicated.

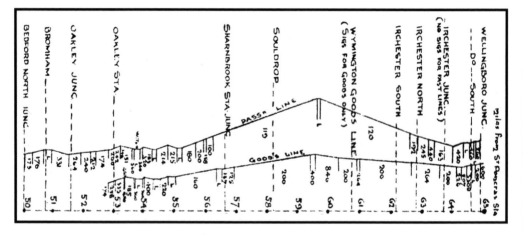

HISTORICAL BACKGROUND

When the Midland Railway was formed in 1844 it inherited the Midland Counties line from Leicester to Rugby which had been opened on 30th June 1840. This gave it an outlet to London via the London & Birmingham Railway (London & North Western from 1846).

Dissatisfaction with the Rugby route and Great Northern support for an extension from Bedford to a junction with its main line to King's Cross led to new proposals. A late change was to proceed to Hitchin instead of Arlesey to join the GNR. This added three extra miles. A Bill was passed on 4th August 1853, the route diverging from the Rugby line at Wigston and reaching Hitchin via Wellingborough and Bedford. The contract for building the line was let to Thomas Brassey with John Knowles of Shefford responsible for only tunnel on the line, Warden, between Cardington and Southill. Financial stringency dictated various money saving features, including in the section covered, climbs of 1 in 120 for coal trains in the up direction south of Irchester and Cardington. The former remained on the main line after the MR London Extension was built, but was eventually bypassed for goods traffic by the Wymington deviation. The River Ouse was crossed no less than seven times south of Sharnbrook and three of the original viaducts required replacing within 35 years, another indication of initial economy. The intermediate stations were built to a common design by C.H.Driver but the materials used varied with location. At Bedford, south of the final crossing of the Ouse, the LNWR branch from Bletchley was crossed on the level. The MR proposed a joint station here but LNWR intransigence prevented an agreement and the line from Wigston (south of Leicester) to Hitchin was opened throughout to passengers on 8th May 1857 without a station at Bedford. Instead a temporary connection to the LNWR station was used. The MR station, situated north of the Ouse and an inconvenient one mile or more from the LNWR establishment, was finally opened on 1st February 1859.

Midland trains ran through to King's Cross from 1st February 1858 but the Rugby line retained its importance. The proportions of the coal tonnage carried by the various routes from the MR to London in 1862 were:

	Tons
Via Rugby and LNWR	491,500
Via Peterborough and Eastern Counties Ry	110,000
Via Nottingham and GNR	99,000
Via Hitchin	117,500
Total	818,000

Eventually the MR decided to build its own line to London and the Extension from Bedford was opened to local passengers on 13th July 1868, followed by main line trains to St Pancras on 1st October. Goods trains had been running for twelve months previously. The Extension had the effect of reducing the status of the Bedford to Hitchin section to a country branch after only eleven years of main line traffic. Incidentally the Wigston to Rugby line suffered similarly. Conversely, the Bedford to Wellingborough section became part of a trunk route to London. It was quadrupled in stages over the period 1883 to 1893, including the Wymington deviation which was opened on 4th May 1884. Sharnbrook Tunnel formed part of the deviation and, with the adoption of independent levels for new goods lines, the 1 in 120 gradient of the passenger lines was reduced to nothing steeper than 1 in 200 for loaded coal trains.

The Bedford & Northampton Railway was promoted independently and received its Act in 1865. It was always worked by the MR with which it was amalgamated in 1886. It was opened to all traffic from Oakley Junction to a new terminus at Northampton (later suffixed St John's Street) on 10th June 1872. The Midland Railway (Additional Powers) Act of 1890 authorised a branch from Irchester Junction to Raunds. There was no actual construction beyond Higham Ferrers. Goods working commenced in 1893 and the branch was opened to passengers on 1st May 1894.

The opening of the Higham Ferrers branch completed the development of the lines covered in this volume. For over forty years there was little change apart from the singling of most of the Bedford to Hitchin line and part of the Northampton branch. This period included the incorporation of the Midland Railway into the London Midland & Scottish from 1st January 1923. In 1939, a simple alteration which was long overdue permitted trains from Bedford to run directly into the main ex-LNWR Northampton Castle station and St John's Street was closed. The lines concerned became part of the London Midland Region of the nationalised British Railways in 1948. There were no further closures of stations to passengers until that of Oakley on 15th September 1958. From then onwards local pasenger services were gradually withdrawn, notably Wellingborough to Higham Ferrers on 15th June 1959, Bedford to Hitchin on 1st January 1962 and Bedford to Northampton on 5th March 1962. Bedford station was resited over a period from 1978 with a completely new structure. No trace remains of the 1859 edifice. So of the fifteen MR stations covered in this volume, only one, Wellingborough, is still open. After privatisation in 1996 the Bedford/Wellingborough passenger service was operated by Midland Main Line.

Over the years some serious accidents have occurred on the main line between Bedford and Wellingborough. These are illustrated together with a 1960 collision on the Northampton branch. The Hitchin line was not immune in its early days, with collisions at the junction with the GNR in 1862 and between a goods train and a rashly shunted mixed train at Shefford in 1889.

PASSENGER SERVICES

The first service on the newly opened line from Leicester to Hitchin in 1857 was surprisingly sparse. One goods and four passenger trains ran in each direction, two of the latter were semi-fast and two called at all stations. Traffic increased when Midland trains commenced to run through to King's Cross in February 1858. Just before the opening of the London Extension in 1868, there were ten up MR trains to King's Cross, local traffic on the GNR was not conveyed. Four served intermediate stations between Bedford and Hitchin, five were non-stop from Bedford and one, the 6.15 p.m. from Leicester, non-stop from Wellingborough. From 1868, the Hitchin service was reduced to a basic four trains in each direction, a pattern which was not broken for ninety years until the introduction of railbuses. There were typically six return journeys daily on the Northampton branch. Between the wars there was a through working to St Pancras. The 1927/8 times were: Northampton dep. 7.35am Bedford arr. 8.23 dep. 8.27 , St Pancras arr. 10.5. The terminus at Northampton, later St John's Street, was also used by MR trains from Wellingborough exercising running powers over the LNWR and providing connections northwards from Wellingborough. There were ten non-stop return trips in 1903. After grouping calls were made at the ex-LNWR stations en route.

The local stations on the main line north of Bedford were well served over the years with some nine trains in each direction calling on weekdays. This frequency was maintained even in the austerity period of the late 1940s but was reduced to four trains in the 1950s before closures took effect.

The best timings were reserved for the longer non-stop runs, but in 1913, Wellingborough had a train which reached St Pancras in 75 minutes after slipping a carriage at Luton. Services stagnated after WW1 until the radical accelerations of 1937 which connected Wellingborough and St Pancras with non-stop trains in 64 minutes (up) and 65 minutes (down). After WWII, such timings were never repeated by steam traction but diesel locomotives were responsible for working bookings of 65 minutes (including ten minutes recovery) up and 56½ minutes down. In the winter of 1982 HSTs appeared and took over the Inter City services in May 1983. The timetable, with apparently random intermediate stops, was not conducive to shorter journeys, a situation which was not rectified until the introduction of the class 170 Turbostars by Midland Main Line in May 1999. Wellingborough is now linked to St Pancras by half hourly 170s taking less than 60 minutes, supplemented by occasional HSTs with a best time of 43 minutes.

Branch Services

The Hitchin-Bedford section had four weekday trains for most of the 19th century, this increasing to five by 1920. In the final year there were seven.

Bedford-Northampton passengers were offered five trains on most weekdays until by 1920 there were six. The 1961 timetable showed nine, with an extra one on Saturdays.

The Higham Ferriers branch had six trains initially, but figures of up to 12 were common in the 20th century. There were three extra on Saturdays in the final year.

There were no Sunday services in the years sampled.

BEDFORD and HITCHIN.—Midland.

Station Street,	Week Days. mrn	mrn	aft	aft	
DERBY 165 ....dep	5 25	8 35	1225	3 10	....
165 NOTTINGHAM ... ,,	5 25	8 40	1230	3 15	....
LEICESTER 165. ,,	6 35	9 45	1 45	4 20	....
165 NORTHAMPTON.. ,,	7 10	1050	2 20	5 20	....
Up.	1&2 clss	1&2 gov	1&2 clss	1&2 gov	
	mrn	aft	aft	aft	
Bedford............dep	8 20	1210	4 0	6 50	....
Cardington	8 26	1216	4 6	6 56	....
Southill................	8 37	1227	4 17	7 7	....
Shefford	8 43	1233	4 23	7 13	....
Henlow.................	8 50	1240	4 30	7 20	....
Hitchin 106,101,100 arr	9 0	1250	4 40	7 30	....
106 LONDON King's C. a	1010	3 35	5 35	9 5	....

King's Cross Station,	Week Days. mrn	mrn	aft	aft
LONDON 106....dep	....	8 5	1 15	4 25
Down.	1&2 gov	1&2 clss	1&2 gov	1&2 clss
	mrn	mrn	aft	aft
Hitchin............dep	7 25	9 20	2 35	5 30
Henlow................	7 32	9 27	2 42	5 37
Shefford	7 39	9 34	2 49	5 44
Southill	7 45	9 40	2 55	5 50
Cardington	7 56	9 51	3 6	6 1
Bedford 162, 120..arr	8 5	10 0	3 15	6 10
162 NORTHAMPTON ..arr	10 5	1150	5 0	9 35
LEICESTER 162. ,,	11 5	1117	5 33	7 55
162 NOTTINGHAM ... ,,	1210	1210	6 30	8 50
DERBY 163 .... ,,	1218	1218	6 30	8 55

1869

BEDFORD and NORTHAMPTON.—Midland.

Fares.

Mls	Single 1 cl.	Single 2 cl.	Single gov	Return 1 cl	Return 2 cl	New Station,	mrn	mrn	aft	aft	aft
—						Northampton ......dep	8 15	9 45	1250	4 35	6 20
6	1 2	0 10	0 6	2 0	1 5	Horton	a	a	1 2	a	6 32
11	2 0	1 6	0 11	3 6	2 6	Olney	8 33	10 3	1 12	4 54	6 42
15½	2 9	2 0	1 3½	4 9	3 6	Turvey	8 42	1012	1 22	5 4	6 52
21½	3 9	2 10	1 9½	6 3	4 9	Bedford 181, 132, 179 a	8 54	1023	1 35	5 15	7 5
37¾	6 9	5 0	3 1½	11 3	8 6	HITCHIN 181 ...arr	....	1252	4 55	....	7 48
71¼	11 6	8 9	5 3½	19 3	14 9	179 LONDON (St.Pan.) ,,	1030	1150	2 55	6 40	8 55

St. Pancras Station,	mrn	mrn	mrn	aft	aft
LONDON 176....dep	8 20	10 0	1145	3 20	5 30
HITCHIN 181.... ,,	7 5	10 0	aft	2 35	6 0
Bedford ....dep	9 45	1115	1 10	4 45	6 55
Turvey	9 57	1126	1 22	4 56	7 7
Olney	10 7	1136	1 32	5 6	7 17
Horton	1017	a	1 42	a	7 27
Northampton 123, 125a	1030	1155	1 53	5 25	7 40

☞ Through Carriages between Northampton and London. a Stop when required.

1873

BEDFORD and HITCHIN.—Midland.

Miles from Bedford.	Week Days only.	mrn	mrn	mrn (Tuesdays and Saturdays)	aft	aft	aft (Saturdays only)
	462 London (St. Pan.).dep.	2 30	7 20	9 30	1215	3 35	6 5
	447 LEICESTER ¶ ...... ,,	....	6 30	9 45	1135	4 17	4 55
—	Bedford..............dep.	6 20	8 54	1112	1 38	5 50	7 42
3	Cardington..............	6 29	9 2	1120	1 46	5 58	7 50
7¼	Southill	6 39	9 11	1129	1 55	6 9	7 59
9¼	Shefford.................	6 48	9 17	1135	2 1	6 15	8 5
12	Henlow ....[293	6 55	9 24	1142	2 8	6 25	8 12
16¼	Hitchin 276, 236, arr.	7 3	9 32	1150	2 16	6 33	8 20
48¼	286 London (K.C.)....arr.	8 41	11A25	1 20	4 0	8 12	1012

Miles	Week Days only.	mrn	mrn	mrn (Tuesdays and Saturdays)	aft	aft	aft (Saturdays only)
	284 London (King's C.)dep.	5 10	8 45	1032	1 10	5 45	8 0
—	Hitchin ....dep.	7 25	10 0	1215	2 42	7 0	9 10
4½	Henlow	7 34	10 8	1224	2 53	7 9	9 19
6¼	Shefford.................	7 40	1014	1230	2 59	7 15	9 25
9	Southill	7 47	1020	1237	3 6	7 22	9 32
13½	Cardington ....[463	7 56	1028	1246	3 15	7 31	9 41
16¼	Bedford * 356a, 438, arr.	8 2	1033	1252	3 21	7 41	9 47
65¼	438 LEICESTER ¶ ......arr.	1050	1210	2 27	6 3	11c0	....
66	463 London (St. Pan.). ,,	9 38	1227	3 30	5 25	10 25	....

A Arrives at 11 15 mrn. on Tuesdays. c Except Saturdays. * Over 1 mile to L. & N. W. Station. ¶ London Road.

BEDFORD and NORTHAMPTON.—Midland.

Miles	Down. Week Days only.	mrn	mrn	mrn	aft	aft	aft
	462 London (St. Pan.)..dep.	2 30	7 20	9 30	1215	2 13	6 5
—	Bedford..............dep.	6 0	8 48	1120	1 50	4 35	7 50
6	Turvey....................	....	9 2	1134	2 4	4 48	8 4
10½	Olney......................	6 47	9 14	1147	2 17	5 2	8 17
15½	Piddington	....	9 25	1158	2 28	5 13	8 28
21½	Northampton 324....arr.	7 5	9 36	12 9	2 39	5 24	8 39

Miles	Up. Week Days only.	mrn	mrn	aft	aft	aft
—	Northampton.........dep.	7 40	9 55	1243	5 50	9 10
6	Piddington	7 53	10 8	1256	6 3	S
11	Olney	8 4	1019	1 7	6 14	9 35
15½	Turvey	8 14	1029	1 15	6 25	S
21½	Bedford * 356a, 463 ..arr.	8 28	1041	1 34	6 37	9 57
71½	463 London (St. Pan.)..arr.	1035	1227	3 30	1025	....

S Stops at Piddington and Turvey on Saturdays only. * Over 1 mile to L. & N. W. Station.

1920

BEDFORD and HITCHIN

Miles	Week Days only	a.m		E		S		am		am		E		S		p.m		E	S	
	218 London (St. P.)...dep	4 25	..	7A15	..	7A15	..	9 25	..	10A35	..	1255	..	1A 5	..	2A35	..	4 30	4 40	..
—	Bedford (Mid. Rd.)..dep	6 20	..	8 45	..	8 45	..	10 47	..	12 22	..	2 30	..	2 30	..	4 28	..	5 59	6 5	..
3	Cardington..............	6 25	..	8 50	..	8 50	..	10 52	..	12 27	..	2 35	..	2 35	..	4 33	..	6 4	6 10	..
7½	Southill...................	6 32	..	8 57	..	8 57	..	10 59	..	12 34	..	2 42	..	2 42	..	4 40	..	6 11	6 17	..
9½	Shefford	6 37	..	9 2	..	9 2	..	11 4	..	12 39	..	2 47	..	2 47	..	4 45	..	6 16	6 22	..
12	Henlow Camp	6 42	..	9 7	..	9 7	..	11 9	..	12 44	..	2 52	..	2 52	..	4 50	..	6 21	6 27	..
16¼	Hitchin ....arr	6 50	..	9 19	..	9 19	..	11 17	..	12 53	..	3 2	..	3 2	..	4 58	..	6 30	6 35	..
48¼	London (K. C.) ....arr	8 0	..	10B33	..	1033	..	12‡41	..	2H 8	..	4 5	..	4B 6	..	6 4	..	7 26	7 41	..

Miles	Week Days only	E		S		am		E		S	E		S	p.m		E	S		p.m
	London (King's C.) dep	6 10	..	6 25	..	8 25	..	10 40	..	10 40	11 30	..	12 25	2T30	..	4 20	4 30	..	5K53
—	Hitchin..............dep	7 35	..	7 35	..	9 45	..	11 47	..	11 47	1 20	..	1 25	3 45		5 21	5 27	..	7 0
4½	Henlow Camp	7 42	..	7 42	..	9 52	..	11 54	..	11 54	1 27	..	1 32	3 52	..	5 28	5 34	..	7 7
6¾	Shefford	7 47	..	7 47	..	9 57	..	11 59	..	11 59	1 32	..	1 37	3 57	..	5 33	5 39	..	7 12
9	Southill	7 51	..	7 51	..	10 2	..	12 3	..	12 3	1 36	..	1 41	4 1	..	5 37	5 44	..	7 16
13¼	Cardington	7 58	..	7 58	..	10 8	..	12 10	..	12 10	1 43	..	1 48	4 8	..	5 44	5 50	..	7 23
16¼	Bedford D..........arr	8 4	..	8 4	..	10 14	..	12 16	..	12 16	1 49	..	1 54	4 17	..	5 52	5 56	..	7 29
66	218 London (St. P.) ..arr	9A40	..	9A38	..	12A12	..	2A10	..	1A47	3A 8	..	3A 8	5∥20	..	7A12	7A30	..	9A 8

A Second class only between London and Bedford
B Second class only between Hitchin and London
D Midland Road; over 1 mile to St. John's Station

E Except Saturdays
H Arr 2 14 pm on Saturdays
K Dep 5 40 pm on Saturdays

S Saturdays only
T Dep 2B30 pm on Saturdays

∥ 4 minutes later on Saturdays

‡ Arr 6 minutes *earlier* on Saturdays

1961

BEDFORD and NORTHAMPTON

Miles	Week Days only	a.m	a.m		a.m	a.m		S	A E	S		p.m	p.m		p.m	p.m	
	218 London (St. Pan.) dep	4 25	6 40	..	8 35	9 35	..	11 25	1135	12 2	..	1 35	3 35	..	5P39	7 5	..
	Bedford (Mid. Rd.)..dep	6 37	8 10	..	9 50	11 26	..	12 38	1 17	1 23	..	3 20	4 48	..	6 53	8 35	..
6	Turvey	6 47	8 24	..	10 0	11 36	..	12 49	1 27	1 33	..	3 30	4 58	..	7 3	8 45	..
10½	Olney	6 55	8 32	..	10 8	11 44	..	12 57	1 35	1 41	..	3 38	5 6	..	7 11	8 53	..
15½	Piddington	..	..	..	1016	11 52	..	1 11	1 43	1 49	..	3 46	..	..	..	..	..
21½	Northampton (Bdge St.)	7 12	8 48	..	1025	12 1	..	1 22	1 52	2 0	..	3 55	5 21	..	7 26	9 8	..
22½	(Castle)arr	7 16	8 51	..	1028	12 4	..	1 26	1 55	2 3	..	3 58	5 25	..	7 30	9 12	..

Miles	Week Days only	a.m	a.m		a.m		p.m	p.m	S A	p.m	p.m		p.m	p.m	
	Northampton (Castle) dp	7 56	9 5	..	10 35	..	1212	2 25	3 30	4 2	6 7	..	7 40	9 20	..
1	,, (Bdge. St.)	7 58	9 7	..	10 37	..	1214	2 27	3 32	4 4	6 9	..	7 42	9 22	..
7½	Piddington	..	9 16	..	10 46	..	1223	2 36	3 41	..	..	..	..	..	..
12	Olney	8 14	9 24	..	10 54	..	1231	2 44	3 49	4 20	6 25	..	7 58	9 38	..
16½	Turvey	8 25	9 32	..	11 2	..	1239	2 52	3 57	4 28	6 33	..	8 6	9 46	..
22½	Bedford (Mid. Rd.)..arr	8 39	9 44	..	11 13	..	1250	3 6	4 11	4 39	6 44	..	8 17	9 57	..
72½	218 London (St. Pan.) arr	9 55	11 7	..	12B55	..	2 10	5 14	5 24	5 56	8 17	..	9 57	1145	..

E Except Saturdays
B Arr 12 30 pm on Saturdays
P Dep 5 35 pm on Saturdays
p pm
S Saturdays only

A Second class only

'61

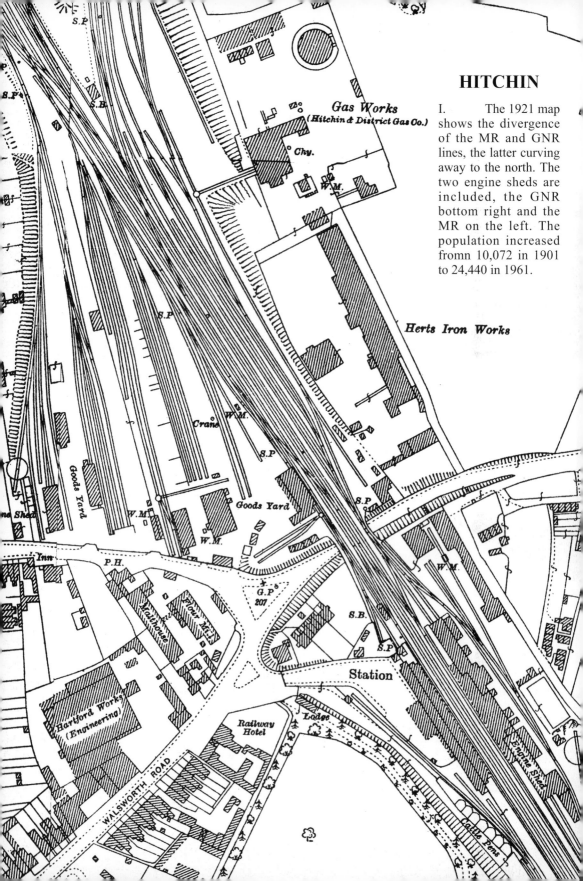

HITCHIN

I.   The 1921 map shows the divergence of the MR and GNR lines, the latter curving away to the north. The two engine sheds are included, the GNR bottom right and the MR on the left. The population increased fromn 10,072 in 1901 to 24,440 in 1961.

S.P.

S.B.

S.P.

Gas Works
(Hitchin & District Gas Co.)

Chy.

W.M.

Herts Iron Works

S.P.

Crane   W.M.

S.P.

ne Shed

Goods Yard

W.M.

Goods Yard

S.P.

W.M.

W.M.

Inn

P.H.

W.M.

G.P
207

Malthouse

Flour Mill

S.B.

S.P.

Hartford Works
(Engineering)

Station

Railway
Hotel

Lodge

Engine Shed

WALSWORTH ROAD

Cattle Pens

1.   Johnson 2-4-0 no.257 stands in the up platform on 29th August 1932, having arrived from Bedford with a three-coach train, which included two ex-MR clerestory vehicles. Despite the MR's reduced status after 1868, its passenger bookings at Hitchin rose steadily from 13,948 in 1873 to 23,091 in 1922. (G.W.Goslin coll.)

2.   Twenty three years later little has changed in the surroundings. On 9th July 1955, we see taper boiler 2-6-2T no.40165 on arrival from its home startion of Bedford with the more usual two coach set. In the absence of bay roads at Hitchin, trains from Bedford had to cross the East Coast Main Line fast lines to reach the up platform. They could be admitted by a calling on arm to an already occupied platform road and thus maintain an onward connection. (R.A.Panting)

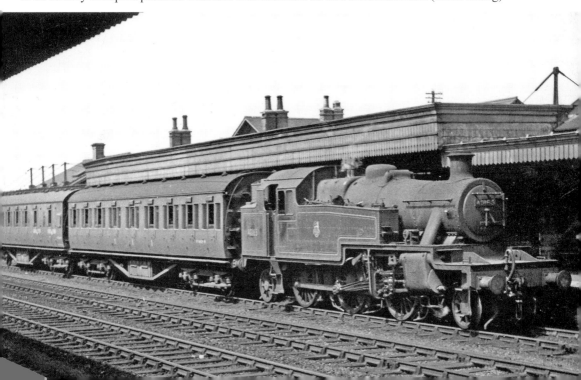

3.   The Bedford to Hitchin and Northampton services were among the earliest MR push and pull workings, first shown in the Working timetable from 1st July 1908. Always known as Motor Trains, they were discontinued in 1917, but were subsequently re-introduced by the LMS in the 1930s. 0-4-4T no.1242 is about to leave for Bedford with one carriage leading and two trailing. The MR's intention was to have the engine sandwiched betwen the carriages, but the LMS stipulated that the engine must lead towards Hitchin. (Lens of Sutton coll.)

4.   30th December 1961 was the last day of the passenger service on the line from Bedford. The signalman at Hitchin Goods Yard signal box collects the Shefford/Hitchin tablet. Despite its full title, the nameboard on the box merely read Hitchin. (K.C.H.Fairey)

5.   Also on 30th December 1961, we look back from the rear of a train from Bedford joining the ECML. Cambridge Junction's home signal from the branch has been pulled off for the train. This and the distant below were the last remaining somersault arms in the district. Hitchin Goods Yard signal box is on the left. The last passenger train was hauled by 2-6-2T no.84005, with Driver Wilf Johnson, Fireman Fred Beales and Guard George Pickford. (K.C.H.Fairey)

6.   Goods traffic on the Hitchin line continued after the withdrawl of pasenger services until 30th December 1963 when traffic ceased between Hitchin and Shefford. In August 1962, 3F 0-6-0 no. 43428 waits to leave the Eastern Region up platform with a single van. The load to Bedford would probably have been augmented at the yard on the down side. The last through working was on 28th December 1963 when D5380 took 15 wagons of bricks and two brake vans from Bedford to Hitchin and returned with the vans. As an unfortunate acknowledgement of the end of the line, the Leicester Railway pub in Nightingale Road, Hitchin, prosaically became The Nightingale in late 1963. (Photomatic)

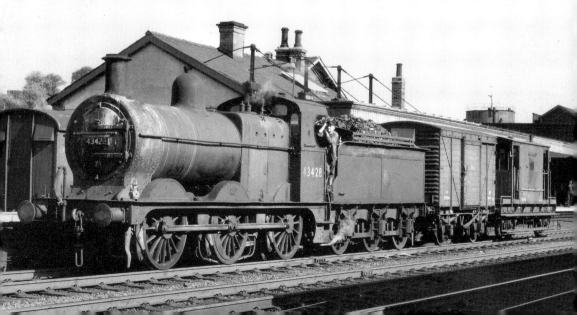

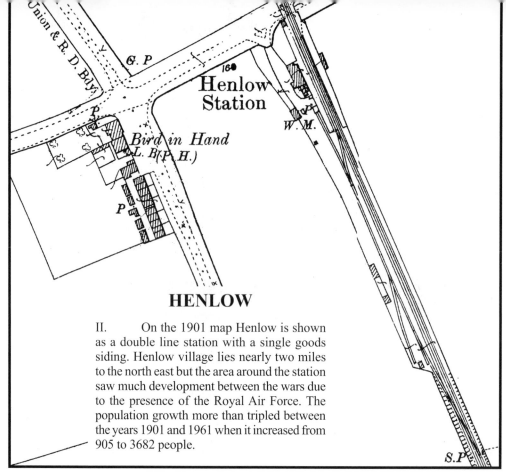

HENLOW

II.   On the 1901 map Henlow is shown as a double line station with a single goods siding. Henlow village lies nearly two miles to the north east but the area around the station saw much development between the wars due to the presence of the Royal Air Force. The population growth more than tripled between the years 1901 and 1961 when it increased from 905 to 3682 people.

7.   A pre-grouping view looks towards Hitchin. The original down line with its platform was then in use, the rails for the up platform had been lifted in 1911. With the growing importance of traffic generated by the adjacent RAF station, the railway station was renamed Henlow Camp on 1st March 1933. Passenger bookings had increased from 8,062 in 1913 to 27,443 in 1922. Before construction, a list of proposed stations noted Henlow as Mappleshall(sic), i.e the present nearby village of Meppershall. (Lens of Sutton coll.)

8.　　From the level crossing we see the station in a post 1939 view looking towards Hitchin. In 1911, when the line between Hichin and Shefford was singled, the up platform was abandoned and all trains used the down platform on which the main building was sited. From 30th September 1917 to 24th February 1924, Henlow blossomed into a crossing station with both platform lines signalled in each direction. What would have been the up line was reserved for goods traffic and workmen's trains. In 1939, by which time passenger traffic was largely confined to RAF personnel, the single line was slewed from the down to the up platform which was lengthened. The MR signal was "replanted" in a position which would have been foul of the structure gauge of the old line. In later years this could lead to the impression that the transition had been made in earlier times. (Photomatic)

9.　　A train of Quad Arts forming a leave special for the RAF stands in the timber extension to the platform before setting out for Hitchin where class J15 no.65479 will be replaced, probably by a B1, for the journey to King's Cross. Motive power was limited by weight restrictions and 65479 was stationed at Hitchin for some years specially for working the leave trains between there and Henlow Camp. (S.Summerson)

NORTH OF HENLOW

III.   The Hoo brickworks was situated
between Henlow and Shefford, north of an
underbridge which took the main Bedford to
Hitchin road below the railway. Plowman's
Siding was brought into use on 19th
December 1893. The 1901 survey shows
a "signal box", actually a "stage" or ground
frame, providing trailing access from the
down line to sidings from which a tramway
descended to cross the main road and share
the underbridge to reach the brickworks. The
embedded rails across the road were still in
position in the mid-1920s but the 1939 OS
revision showed both brickworks and siding
as "disused" and an "old tramway" only from
the siding to the road.

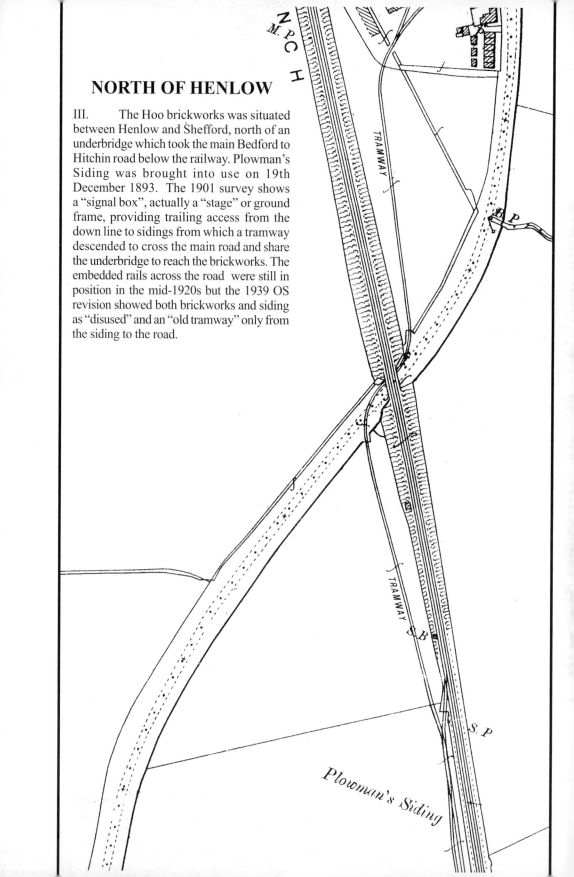

SHEFFORD

IV.   Shefford station, top left in the 1938 survey, was adjacent to the High Street. Passenger bookings at Shefford were remarkably constant, varying from 19,936 in 1883 to 20,234 in 1922. The number of inhabitants grew from 874 people in 1901 to a larger 2216 by 1961.

Green Man (P.H.)

NORTHBRIDGE STREET

TCB

P

Blo

SOUTHBRIDGE STREET

Station

War Meml.

St. Michael's Ch. (Vicarage)

Bedford 9
Hitchin 7

M.P.

Sou
Brid

Railway Inn

HIGH STREET

S.P.

W.M.

St. Francis's Home

F.B.

Cattle Pens

S.B.

S.S.

10. Although the station was conveniently situated for the town, its site, precariously perched on an embankment, caused difficulties. The original buildings on the down platform are seen to be supported by massive timber shores. (J.Osgood)

11. Increasing dilapidation of the timber structure led to the provision of a new main building of pre-cast concrete units at street level in 1954. This enabled the weight on the embankment to be reduced, but the building was destined to have a working life of less than eight years. (London Midland Region)

12. Two new 130 foot platforms were provided in 1954. Looking towards Bedford, we see the down platform with its small shelter on 5th May 1955. Much of the timber used in the reconstuction was recovered from Carpenders Park, then being rebuilt to a higher standard. (London Midland Region)

13. Tickets from Hitchin are collected from passengers seen leaving a rail bus. The buses took over from conventional trains on 11th August 1958, running to the existing timetable. On 15th September 1958, the basic service was increased from four to seven return journeys daily and within a month the number of passengers had more than doubled. The rail buses ceased running in November 1959 and were replaced by Derby two-car DMUs. These had to be withdrawn for modification and steam push-pull trains were re-introduced. (J.Osgood)

14.   Class 3F 0-6-0 no.43521 is seen with a goods train from Bedford on 7th November 1962. After traffic to Hitchin ceased, the line to Bedford, worked as "one engine in steam", remained for twelve months until 28th December 1964. The yard had a 5-ton crane. (K.C.H.Fairey)

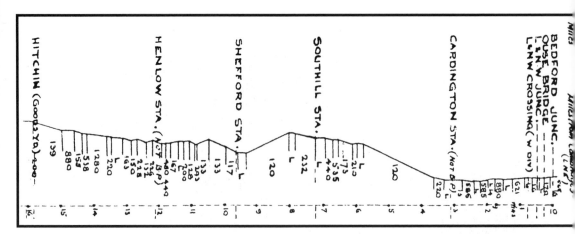

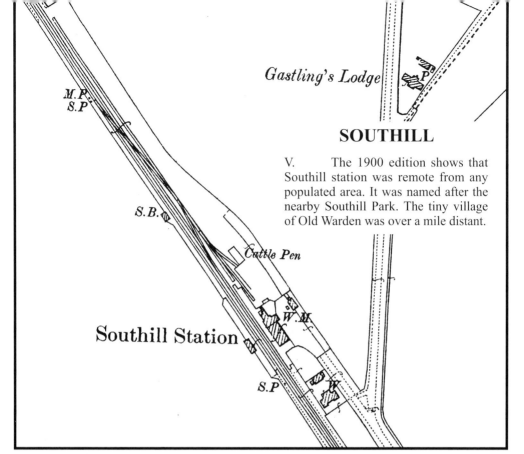

Gastling's Lodge

M.P.
S.P

S.B.

Cattle Pen

SOUTHILL

V.   The 1900 edition shows that Southill station was remote from any populated area. It was named after the nearby Southill Park. The tiny village of Old Warden was over a mile distant.

Southill Station

W.M.

S.P

15.   Looking towards Bedford, we see the elongated station buildings which included a waiting room for use by members of the Whitbread family. William Whitbread was a keen supporter of proposals for the railway and offered land for seven miles of line through his estates at agricultural value. The station was listed as South Hill in a pre-construction document and the Board of Trade Inspection Report noted it as Parkhill. The latter was probably a simple lapse of memory. (Lens of Sutton coll.)

16.   A goods train from Bedford headed by class 3F 0-6-0 no.43521 approaches on 7th November 1962. The signalman waits to take the tablet for the single line section from Bedford St Johns no.1. This section was singled on 19th November 1911, but double line remained onwards to Shefford. (K.C.H.Fairey)

17.   Class 3F 0-6-0 no. 43428 stands with a pick up goods for Bedford on 16th November 1962. On the left is a venerable hand crane and on the right Southill signal box. (K.C.H.Fairey)

18. Southill signal box was photographed in about 1939. The block telegraph had been introduced between Southill and Cardington, a section which included Warden Tunnel, by 1873 (up) and 1876 (down). It was not extended to Hitchin until 3rd June 1890, on which date this box was opened. After the conversion to single line from Cardington it had a frame of fifteen levers, all of which were working.
(G.W.Goslin coll.)

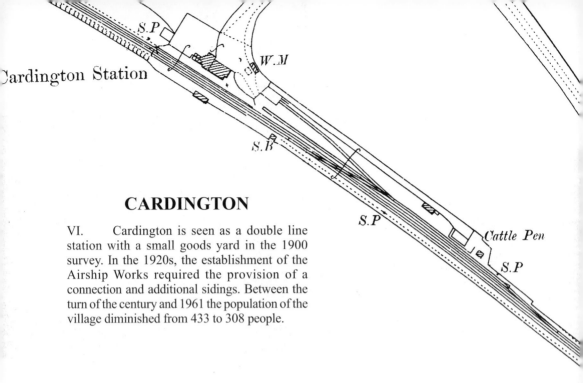

Cardington Station   *S.P*   *W.M*   *S.B*   *S.P*   Cattle Pen   *S.P*

CARDINGTON

VI.　　Cardington is seen as a double line station with a small goods yard in the 1900 survey. In the 1920s, the establishment of the Airship Works required the provision of a connection and additional sidings. Between the turn of the century and 1961 the population of the village diminished from 433 to 308 people.

19.　　The south portal of Warden Tunnel, 882 yards long, marked the end of a two mile climb at 1 in 120 from Cardington, although the general trend southbound was still uphill to beyond Southill. We look over the shoulder of the driver of a railbus to see through the straight bore on 3rd September 1959. (K.C.H.Fairey)

20.   The disused down platform is seen on the left, looking towards Bedford in the 1930s. In general, Cardington had the least passenger traffic of all the stations covered in this volume. Only 3,134 passengers were booked in 1922, about ten each weekday. After the "one engine in steam" goods working to Shefford ceased, Air Ministry traffic was still carried between Bedford and Cardington, the last train running on 4th February 1969. Official closure followed on 28th April 1969. (Lens of Sutton coll.)

21.   Taper boiler 2-6-2T No 165, a long term resident at Bedford, was derailed while shunting at Cardington on 9th April 1940. (Lens of Sutton coll.)

22.   Although it was not a crossing station, Cardington's ground frame gave access to extensive sidings for the RAF station. On 24th June 1939, 0-4-0T *Lord Fisher*, Andrew Barclay no.1399 of 1915, was in use by the Air Ministry Works Dept. The RAF presence at Cardington stemmed from the WW1 aircraft factory of Short Brothers Ltd. (hence Shortstown as a local place name). For workers at the factory, Cardington Workmen's Platform, situated near the Bedford to Hitchin road overbridge at 2 miles 15 chains from Bedford Junction, was in use from about September 1917 to 1921. The gap in the hedge marking the site of the halt could still be seen in the 1930s. (G.W.Goslin coll.)

23.   A late use for the line between Cardington and Warden Tunnel was for filming a scene for "Those Magnificent Men in Their Flying Machines" in May 1964. Jones Goods no.103 came down from Scotland and made runs on the branch disguised as a French locomotive. After all this preparation, she only made a brief appearance in the final production. She is seen on Bedford shed on 10th May 1964. (P.H.Groom)

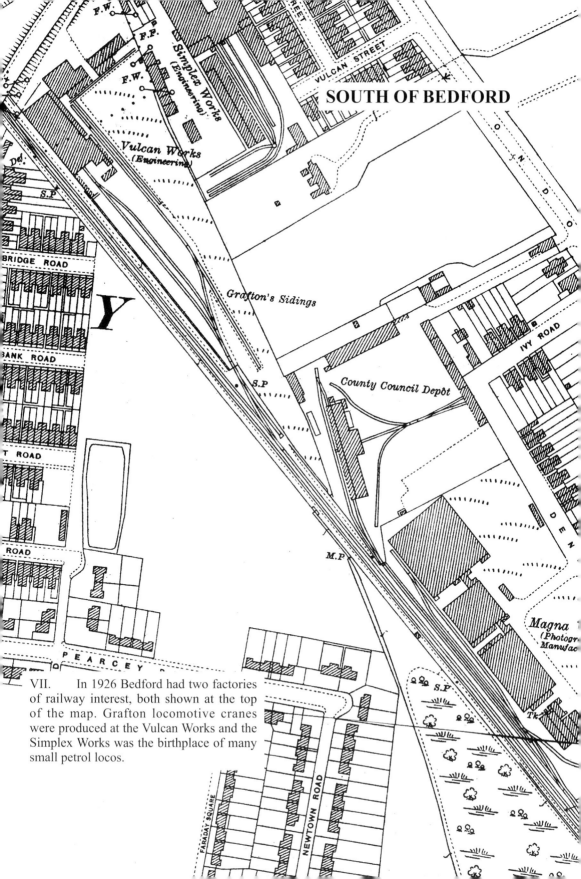

VII. In 1926 Bedford had two factories of railway interest, both shown at the top of the map. Grafton locomotive cranes were produced at the Vulcan Works and the Simplex Works was the birthplace of many small petrol locos.

VIII.
Approaching
Bedford, the
ex-LNWR
Bletchley to
Cambridge
line is crossed
on the level.
This is shown
at the bottom
of the 1926
map with the
LNWR engine
shed, closed
after 1923, on
the right. After
the Bottom
Sidings on the
left and the
malthouses
the connection
from St Johns
station and the
LNWR yard
joins from the
right. From
1901 to 1961
the population
almost
doubled going
from 35,144
to 65,370.

24.   This
is complex
trackwork at
the crossing of
the Hitchin and
Bletchley lines at
Bedford St Johns
no.1 box. We look
right towards
Bletchley and
upwards towards Hitchin. When the line to Southill was singled,
the old up line was retained as a long siding serving factories such as
Grafton's Vulcan Works and Marion & Foulger. A connection from
the siding across the single main line was provided to a factory on
the west side on 17th April 1940. The premises were built for the Co-
operative Wholesale Society as a canning factory, but were occupied
during the war by Pobjoy, an aero engine firm. The connection was
controlled by a ground frame, released by Bedford St Johns no.1
provided that a Bedford to Southill tablet was not "out". Another
wartime addition was made on 15th February 1942. This was a siding
to a Ministry of Food store. Willow Street ground frame controlled
the connection, in this instance from the single running line. An
auxiliary tablet instrument was provided so that a train could be put
inside for another to pass. (G.W.Goslin coll.)

25.   A goods train for Bletchley leaves the ex-LNWR yard,
crosses the Hitchin lines and passes behind Bedford St Johns no.1
box in June 1947. Bedford's 3F 0-6-0 no.3222 is in charge. The
temporary connection into the LNWR station used by Hitchin trains
before 1859 would have crossed the path of the train shown on the
extreme right of this view. The Board of Trade's Inspecting Officer,
Col. Yolland , noted "All trains proceeding from Hitchin to Leicester
have to be backed in, crossing over the up line and all trains from
Leicester to Hitchin have to be pushed out from this station. This
process is objectionable and in my opinion should only be sanctioned
as a temporary arrangement". (Rail Archive Stephenson)

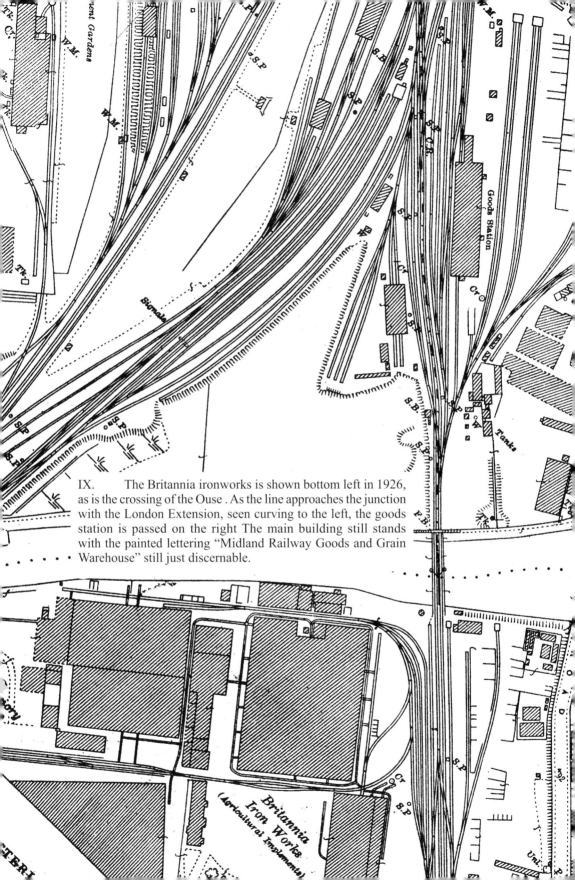

IX. The Britannia ironworks is shown bottom left in 1926, as is the crossing of the Ouse . As the line approaches the junction with the London Extension, seen curving to the left, the goods station is passed on the right The main building still stands with the painted lettering "Midland Railway Goods and Grain Warehouse" still just discernable.

26.   The tablet for the section from Southill is given up at Bedford St Johns no.1 box from 2-6-2T no.40165 on 30th July 1956. (D.K.Jones)

27.   A train of empty wagons approaches Bedford LNW Junction signal box from Hitchin. This box was lower than standard so that the signalman had a good view beneath the adjacent overbridge, which carried the Kempston Road. Block working between Bedford LNW Junction, Ouse Bridge and Bedford Junction was a late introduction, on 25th January 1892. (A.Warrington)

28.   J & F Howard's Britannia Works was the source of considerable rail traffic. Their private sidings diverged at Bedford LNW Junction box. In addition to a Grafton locomotive crane, a Manning Wardle 0-4-0T was used for shunting. Works no.1381 of 1899, it was purchased from the Isle of Axholme Joint Railway in January 1909 and was in use until the closure of the works in the 1930s. Howard's engines worked out of the works into the main line sidings, not always with a good relationship. The *Bedfordshire Times* of 23rd October 1875 reported that "a pointsman [signalman] was fined with costs for assaulting an engine driver employed by J & F Howard by throwing a bucket of soapy water over him as he drove his engine past defendant's signal box". (G.Webb coll.)

29.   As steam traction drew to an end, the last regular workings through Bedford were the coal trains supplying Goldington power station between Bedford and Willington, on the Cambridge line. In the absence of facing points at Bedford LNW Junction, 8F 2-8-0 no.48381 is starting from the down line to traverse the tortuous passage past the ex-LNWR yard to reach Bedford St Johns and the line to Goldington on 31st July 1965. (J.Osgood)

30.　　A train carrying London's refuse to a landfill site at Forder's Sidings, Stewartby, threads its way round the curve from Bedford station headed by no.47367 on 25th April 1990. The load at that time was carried in sheeted open wagons, but sealed containers are now provided. (G.W.Goslin)

31.　　The train　shown in photograph 30 continues over the Ouse, briefly following the original course of the Hitchin line before diverging to join the Bedford to Bletchley branch. In the background is the site of the MR coal yard, closed on 7th June 1969 and now, inevitably, covered by parked cars. (G.W.Goslin)

32.   Ouse Bridge box is seen, looking towards Hitchin. The bridge over the Ouse is immediately beyond the footbridge. The box was closed, together with Bedford LNW Junction, on 16th July 1966. (A.Warrington)

P. F 70
R 2.

Midland Railway.

HITCHIN

33.　　　We look north from the footbridge by the Ouse on 23rd April 1960 to see the top yard and the goods warehouse. All the trap points are open and shunting by "Jinty" no.47549 has been temporarily suspended, probably for the passing of a Bedford to Hitchin passenger train. (S.Summerson)

34.　　　Fowler 2-6-2T no.40026 is seen outside Bedford shed on 22nd February 1962. In the 1940s, engines of this class were used in pairs between Bedford and Cardington to "top and tail" trains taking RAF recruits to Bridgnorth and other destinations. As with the Hitchin to Henlow Camp trains, returning to the token station in the rear was permitted from Cardington to Bedford St Johns no.1 box for such workings. (K.C.H.Fairey)

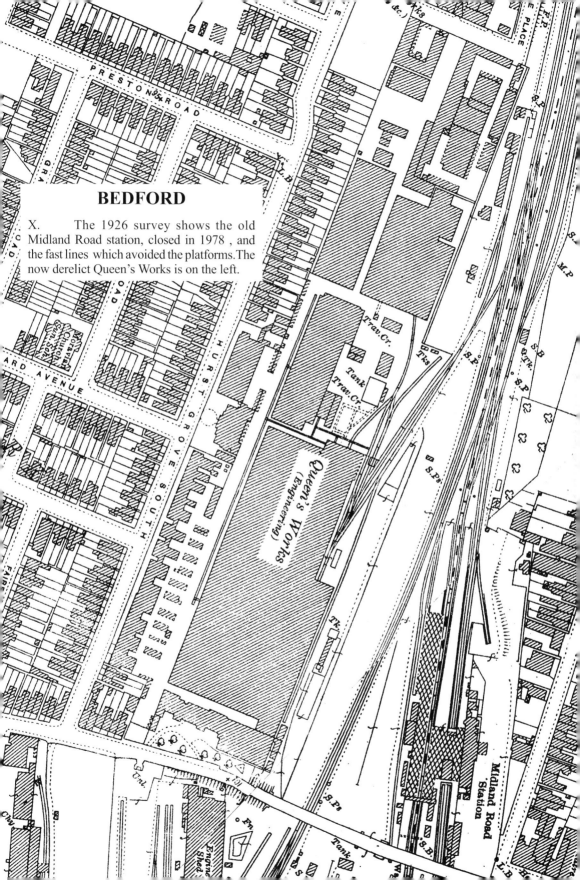

BEDFORD

X.   The 1926 survey shows the old Midland Road station, closed in 1978 , and the fast lines which avoided the platforms. The now derelict Queen's Works is on the left.

35.   Despite the initial lack of a station, the opening of the Leicester & Hitchin Railway was celebrated at Bedford. 200 people were invited to a public dinner at the Assembly Rooms presided over by the Mayor, W.W.Kilpin. The *Bedfordshire Mercury* reported that "Ladies were admitted by special tickets to the gallery where tea and refreshments were provided by way of relief to the somewhat dull privilege of watching the gentlemen dine." Kirtley 0-6-0 no.2645 is seen with a goods train in the up platform of the 1859 station in June 1929. A steam roller is included in the cargo. (LGRP)

36.   2-4-0 no.20251 stands in the down platform road in 1939. Although Johnson's engines were renowned for their graceful outlines, the lack of shelter afforded by their minimal cabs is well shown. (C.R.L.Coles)

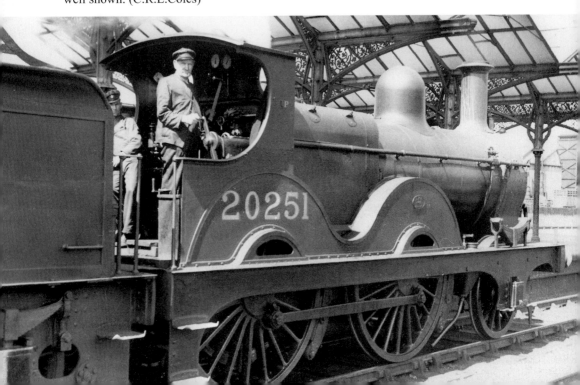

37.   A motor train to Northampton is about to depart from the Wellingborough bay in the late 1950s. (Photomatic)

38.   Railbus no.79971 enters Midland Road station to form the 08.43 to Hitchin on 4th September 1958. Three units, 79971-3, were in use. They were built by Park Royal Vehicles Ltd. with 150 hp engines and seated 46 passengers. (K.C.H.Fairey)

39.   We look south from the footbridge to see BR/Sulzer type 4 no. D134 about to depart from Midland Road for St Pancras with an up express in 1965. The train will take the route to the right. The course of the Hitchin line can be seen through the arch of the bridge. Apart from Bedford, only Wellingborough and Olney of the stations covered in this volume were provided with footbridges between the platforms. (J.Osgood)

40.   Clearance of the site for the new station is in progress in September 1978. We look north to see the fast lines on the left and the old down platform buildings on the right. (G.W.Goslin)

41.　　Platforms 2 and 3 of the new station could not be extended at the northern end to their full length until the old track layout had been revised. Instead a temporary timber extension at the south end, seen here in September 1980, was provided. (G.W.Goslin)

> **Other views of this station can be found in my**
> *St. Albans to Bedford* **album, pictures 96-120.**

SPECIAL CHEAP DAY TICKETS

Return Fares — Second class only

TO and FROM	Bedford Midland Rd.	Cardington	Southill	Shefford	Henlow Camp	Hitchin
	s. d.	s. d.	s. d.	s. d.	s. d.	s. d.
Bedford Midland Road..	---	1/-	2/-	2/6	3/3	4/3
Cardington ..	1/-	--	---	—	—	3/6
Southill	2/-	---	---	—	—	2/9
Shefford	2/6	—	—	—	—	2/-
Henlow Camp	3/3	---	---	—	—	1/6
Hitchin	4/3	3/6	2/9	2/-	1/6	—

Available outward and return by any train the same day

Staffords, Netherfield

42.   Bedford North signal box and we look south east on 6th May 1975. The lines immediately in front of the box are from the carriage sidings. It was replaced by a temporary box situated immediately to its north in November 1978 during the complex changeover of the permanent way from the old to the new stations. (N.D.Mundy)

43.   A Johnson Single Driver heads an up express on the fast lines avoiding the speed restricted platform roads in about 1904. The signals seen were unchanged fifty years later except for the provision of upper quadrant arms. (NRM/P.C.Dewhurst coll.)

44. Another Johnson Single Driver has traversed the connection to the slow lines to bring an express into the up platform in about 1900. The line in the left foreground is the exit from the Northampton bay. The track is laid in the old Midland style with the keys inside the rails. This required the fouling bar for the facing points to be located against the outside face of the rail. (NRM/Tripp coll.)

45. Bromham box, opened on 20th July 1902, between Bedford and Oakley Junction had running junctions from up goods to up passenger and down passenger to down goods lines. This enabled goods trains to use the fast lines through Bedford thereby avoiding obstruction of the platform lines. The box was closed on 19th February 1967, due to the decline in goods traffic. (A.Warrington)

46. For many years a train of empty milk vans passed through Bedford in the afternoon. It is seen on the down goods line at Bromham box in 1928 with Class 3 4-4-0 no.756. The six leading vehicles are old six wheeled carriages, possibly en route to Derby for scrapping. (LGRP)

47. Class 5 4-6-0 no.44983 is seen with a down express north of Bromham viaduct in August 1952. The two leading coaches are an experimental articulated pair. (G.W.Goslin)

48.　　The original Bromham Viaduct, seen looking west on 4th May 1889, consisted of a long timber portion of short spans across the flood plain of the Ouse and an iron girder span for the river crossing. A more substantial structure was built alongside and brought into use in 1890 for the goods lines. Passenger traffic was diverted over the new viaduct in 1891 to enable a replacement to be provided. Four track working over the two new viaducts commenced on 14th February 1892. (British Railways)

49.　　Oakley Junction signal box was the point of divergence of the Northampton branch. We see the replacement box, which was opened on 12th December 1937. It had a 50-lever frame and an illuminated track diagram was provided in place of individual track circuit indicators, a considerable novelty locally. The box was closed on 10th May 1970, some six years after branch goods traffic had ceased on 20th January 1964. Passenger services had previously been withdrawn on 5th March 1962. On 27th June 1918, King George V and Queen Mary paid a visit to Bedford. The Royal Train from St Pancras arrived in the up platform having set back from the down fast line over clipped points. After morning engagements Their Majesties left Bedford at 1.30 p.m. for Oakley Junction at which isolated spot they took lunch, with the Royal Train standing on the down Northampton line. The engine ran round via the down sidings and the train left for Bedford at 2.50 p.m. for an afternoon visit to Bedford School. The engine of the Royal Train must have worked tender first in one direction either to or from Oakley Junction. (A.Warrington)

50.   On 21st January 1938, the 2.10 p.m. express from St Pancras to Bradford collided with a train of empty coaches standing on the down Northampton line at Oakley Junction. The express had been irregularly accepted from Bromham box as the empty coach train occupied a track circuit which prevented the signalman from setting his points for the down passenger line. Despite the higher speeds that were necessary since the accelerations of the previous year there had been no alterations to the signals and the down distant was only 743 yards in the rear of the home signal. The express overran the latter, continued on to the branch and collided with the empty coach train. (L.Hanson)

51.   The express was headed by Jubilee no.5568 *Western Australia*. She is seen minus bogie and middle cylinder after separation from the wreckage. Two passengers and a member of the restaurant car staff were killed. (L.Hanson)

52.   The engine of the empty coach train was Crab 2-6-0 no. 2893. Damage to the smokebox door indicates the severity of the head-on collsion which destroyed the buffer beam and the front of the frames. (L.Hanson)

53.   Class 8F 2-8-0 no.48180 heads an up coal train at Oakley Junction in August 1952. The sidings on the far side of the passenger lines were used to store excursion stock during the winter months. (G.W.Goslin)

54.   Jubilee class no.45615 *Malay States* with an up express passes Oakley Junction in August 1952. Water is still splashing off the tender after an overflow at Oakley troughs. (G.W.Goslin)

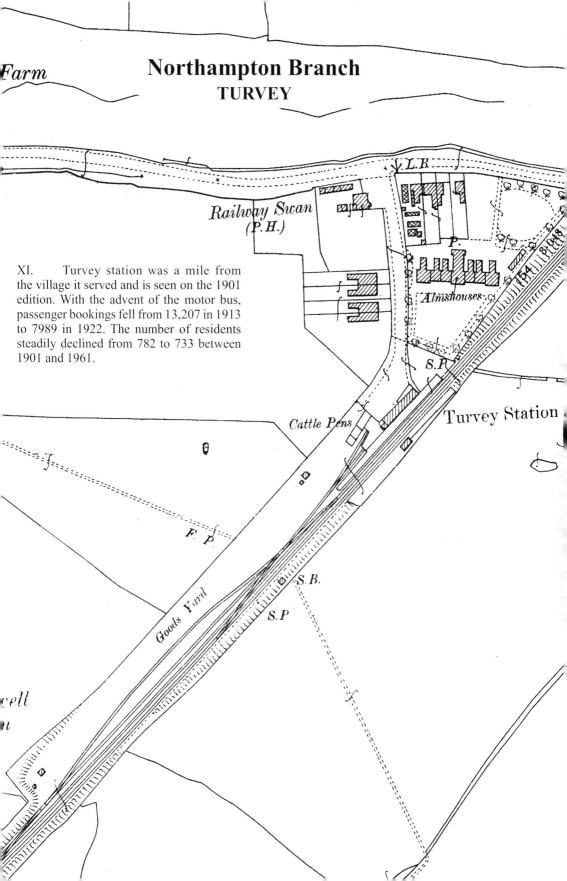

Northampton Branch
TURVEY

Farm

Railway Swan
(P.H.)

L.B.

P.

Almshouses

S.P.

XI.   Turvey station was a mile from the village it served and is seen on the 1901 edition. With the advent of the motor bus, passenger bookings fell from 13,207 in 1913 to 7989 in 1922. The number of residents steadily declined from 782 to 733 between 1901 and 1961.

Cattle Pens

Turvey Station

F P

Goods Yard

S.B.

S.P.

→

56.　　The Olney to Turvey tablet is surrendered from 2-6-2T no.84005 to the signalman on 15th February 1962. In addition to a short period in 1913, the Turvey to Olney section was worked as a single line from 1915, the old down line remaining as a siding. Facing points were not provided at Turvey until 1940 when Government funding was probably available due to WWII. For the intervening 25 years all down trains had to set back at Turvey over the one-time trailing crossover, clipped for passenger workings, to reach the single ex-up line. A story, possibly apocryphal, is told of a new lad at Turvey who was sent out with the clips. After a very bumpy set back, it was found that he had put the clips over rather than under the rails. (K.C.H.Fairey)

55.　　The station is seen looking towards Olney in March 1962, the month in which passenger services were withdrawn from the branch. Class 5 4-6-0 no.44691 stands at the up platform. (Photomatic)

→

57.　　On 17th June 1960, a train of prefabricated track was admitted to the old down line at Turvey, then used to store carriages. The driver misunderstood and thought he was right away to Olney. After about one and a half miles there was a violent collision with the carriages. Class 8F 2-8-0 no.48616 is seen being re-railed four days later. The engine was withdrawn as a result of the damage sustained, the first of the class to go. (K.C.H.Fairey)

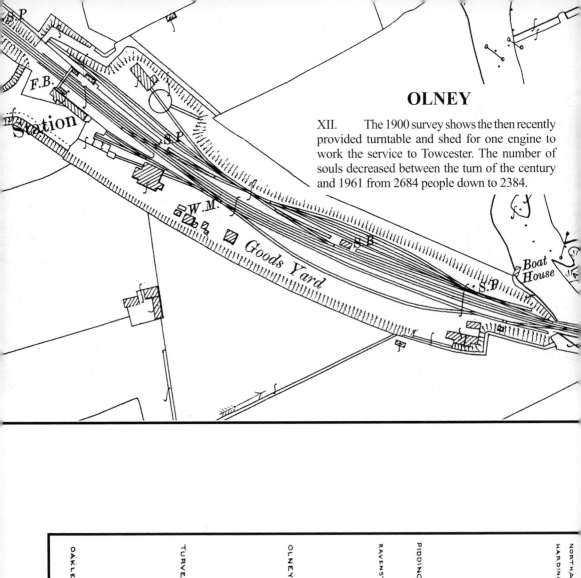

OLNEY

XII.   The 1900 survey shows the then recently provided turntable and shed for one engine to work the service to Towcester. The number of souls decreased between the turn of the century and 1961 from 2684 people down to 2384.

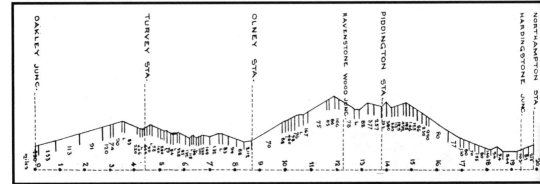

58.	Looking towards Northampton, we see the beginning of the three mile climb to a summit before Ravenstone Wood Junction. The first mile was at 1 in 70 and the whole bank averaged about 1 in 80, a sore trial for down goods trains. (LGRP)

59.	The stone built shelter on the up platform is seen on 3rd March 1962. There were similar structures at Turvey and Piddington. (L.Hanson)

WEST OF OLNEY

60.   The junction at Ravenstone Wood between Olney and Piddington was photographed in April 1952. The ex-Stratford-on-Avon & Midland Junction line to Towcester and, eventually, Broom Junction diverges to the left. The SMJ possessed running powers to Olney and the LMS made use of the route for banana trains from Avonmouth to London. (D.W.F.Goslin)

61.   Ravenstone Wood Junction signal box is seen in April 1952, looking towards Northampton. The box was opened on 29th June 1891 and closed on 27th July 1964. The single line section to Towcester was exceptionally long at 10 miles 1054 yards. (D.W.F.Goslin)

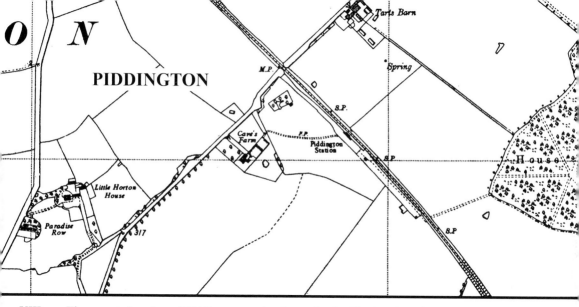

PIDDINGTON

XIII.   The remote location of Piddington station is emphasised in the 1951 six inch to the mile survey. Passenger bookings never reached 10,000 per year and had fallen to 3,634 in 1922. The population of the village was 387 in 1901.

62.   Looking towards Bedford we see the lonely station in about 1950. Piddington was never well patronised although the main buildings were on the same scale as Olney. Opened as Horton, it became Piddington & Horton from 1st May 1876 to 1st April 1904. (B.Cross coll.)

63.   BR Standard 2-6-2T no.84005 leaves Piddington with a Northampton to Bedford train on 15th February 1962. After closure of the branch from Oakley Junction, the line was retained between Piddington to Hardingstone Junction to enable traffic to reach a military depot at Yardley Chase. (K.C.H.Fairey)

64.   The main buildings at Piddington are seen in this view looking towards Northampton. Lack of platform furniture indicates that the photograph was taken soon after the 5th March 1962 closure to passengers. (B.Cross coll.)

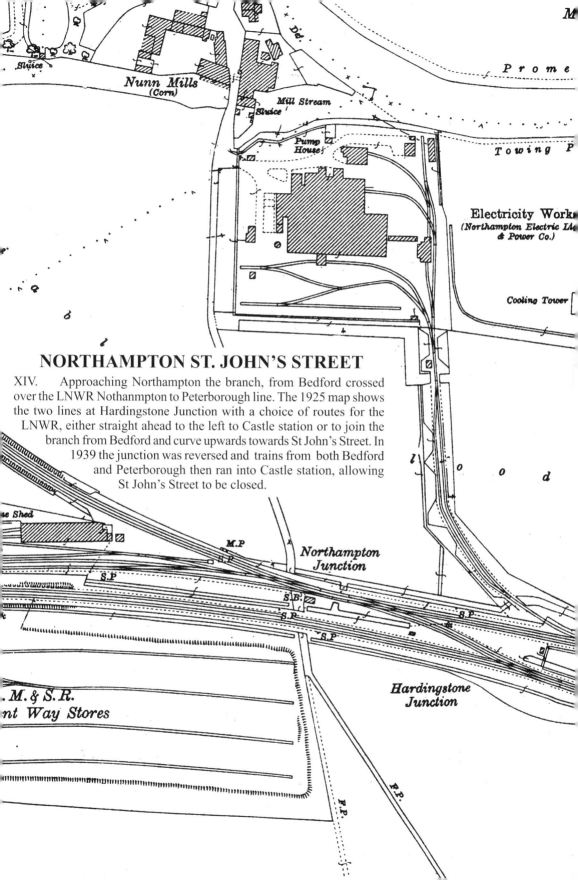

Prome

Nunn Mills
(Corn)

Sluice

Mill Stream
Sluice

Pump
House

Towing P

Electricity Work
(Northampton Electric Li
& Power Co.)

Cooling Tower

NORTHAMPTON ST. JOHN'S STREET

XIV.   Approaching Northampton the branch, from Bedford crossed
over the LNWR Nothanmpton to Peterborough line. The 1925 map shows
the two lines at Hardingstone Junction with a choice of routes for the
LNWR, either straight ahead to the left to Castle station or to join the
branch from Bedford and curve upwards towards St John's Street. In
1939 the junction was reversed and trains from both Bedford and
Peterborough then ran into Castle station, allowing
St John's Street to be closed.

l   *o*   *o*   *d*

Shed

M.P
S.P

*Northampton
Junction*

S.P

S.B.
S.P

S.P

S.P

S.P

S.P

*M. & S.R.
nt Way Stores*

*Hardingstone
Junction*

P.P

P.P

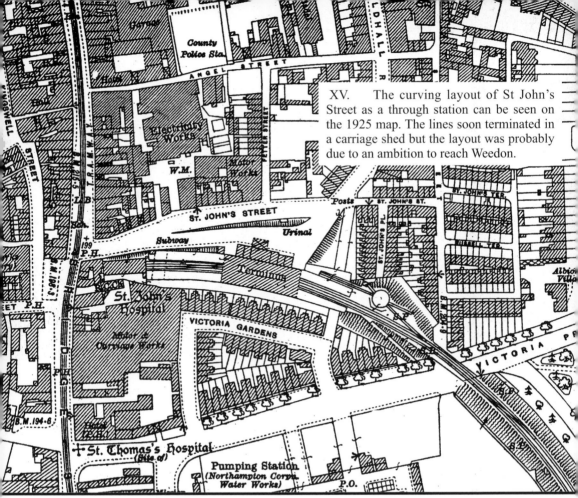

XV.   The curving layout of St John's Street as a through station can be seen on the 1925 map. The lines soon terminated in a carriage shed but the layout was probably due to an ambition to reach Weedon.

65.   From the extensive forecourt we see the massive main building and porte cochere of Northampton St John's Street, opened with the line from Bedford on 10th June 1872. Previously, MR trains from Wellingborough used a terminus near the LNWR station at Bridge Street. Both station and forecourt are examples of the over provision which was to some extent repeated at the intermediate stations. The high pitched roof of the train shed can be seen on the left. Before grouping it was plain Northampton but on 2nd June 1924 it gained its suffix to distinguish it from the main ex-LNWR station which then became Northampton Castle. (Real Photographs)

66.	At St John's Street in the early 1930s, Bedford's 2-4-0 no.256 is about to return home. The double line running through the curved train shed is possibly a reminder of the original intention to extend the line to Weedon. This would not have met with LNWR favour and the Act only authorised the line as far as Northampton. During construction there were further pleas for an extension to Weedon and Daventry and plans for additional stations at Newton Blossomville and Little Houghton, none of which came to fruition. (Photomatic)

67.	Ex-LNWR engines appeared at St John's Street on Wellingborough trains, including no.5023 *Dagmar* on 19th September 1931. After trains from Bedford could run directly into Northampton Castle, the redundant St John's Street was closed on 3rd July 1939. (L.Hanson)

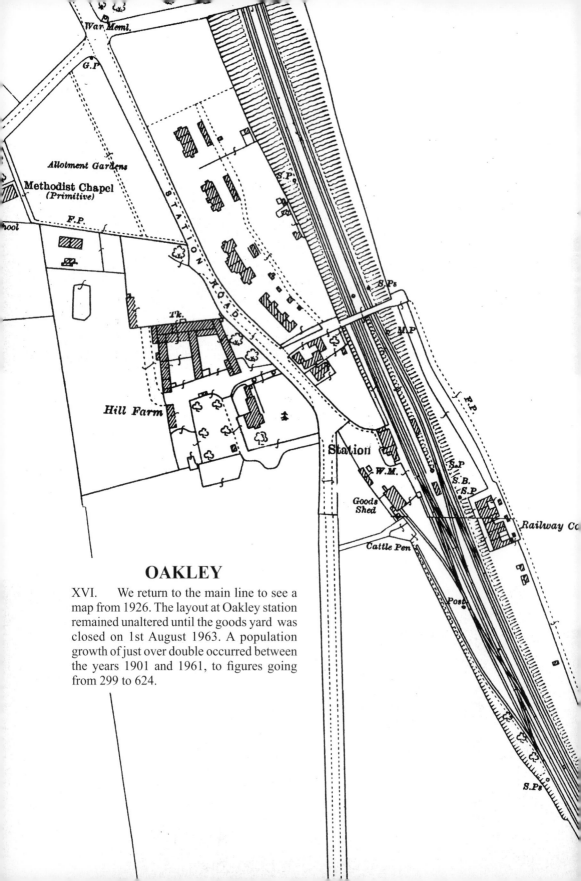

OAKLEY

XVI. We return to the main line to see a map from 1926. The layout at Oakley station remained unaltered until the goods yard was closed on 1st August 1963. A population growth of just over double occurred between the years 1901 and 1961, to figures going from 299 to 624.

68.	Clapham Viaduct is situated between Oakley Junction and Oakley station. The design of the original structure was similar to that of Bromham Viaduct. This view, looking north, is dated 1st May 1888. Its replacement also followed a similar construction sequence to that of Bromham viaduct.	Full four track working over the new structures commenced on 11th September 1892. (British Railways)

69.	Looking south we see that the main building was on the down side. There was no footbridge, passengers for Bedford and the south had to cross both fast lines to reach the up platform. The station was closed to passengers on 15th September 1958. (Lens of Sutton coll.)

70.　　An up coal train collided with the rear of a similar train standing on Oakley Viaduct on 4th October 1949 owing to an obstruction ahead. The Sharnbrook signalman had wrongly thought that "Train Out of Section" had been sent from Oakley station box. The engine and 14 wagons of the second train fell 25 feet from the viaduct, both enginemen being killed instantly. This sad event resulted in the end of the ex-MR "telegraph bell" system which had been used to control the goods lines. (G.W.Goslin coll.)

71.　　Kirtley 800 class 2-4-0 no.62 has just passed over Oakley troughs with an up stopping train in about 1918. (F.W.Goslin)

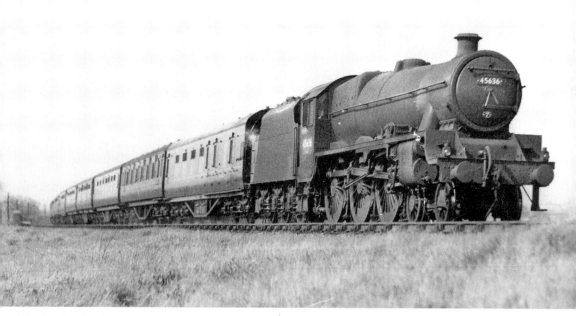

72. Jubilee 4-6-0 no.45636 *Uganda* with an up express has just taken water from the troughs on 18th July 1949. (G.W.Goslin)

73.   Towards the end of WW1 some 4-2-2s were used for assisting coal trains. As in this instance, the single was usually coupled inside, becoming the train engine with a larger pilot. A 4-2-2 assists a coal train headed by Class 4 0-6-0 no.3870 at the south end of Oakley troughs in about 1918. (F.W.Goslin)

74. Compound 4-4-0 no.1040 is on Oakley troughs with an up express in about 1918. (F.W.Goslin)

75. Rebuilt Class 2 4-4-0 no.549 takes water from Oakley troughs with an up express in about 1918. Despite four years of war, the engine is spotlessly turned out complete with burnished buffer heads. The troughs were in use from 5th February 1904 to 5th October 1964. (F.W.Goslin)

76.		North of Oakley we see EWS no.66059 heading a train of empty roadstone wagons bound for Bardon Hill on 11th June 2003. The train is spanning the site of the water troughs which were installed on all four roads. (G.W.Goslin)

77.		A down HST speeds over the site of Oakley troughs on 11th June 2003. The concrete walling provided to prevent erosion of the cutting by water spilled from the troughs is still in situ. (G.W.Goslin)

78.　　Class 2 4-4-0 no.545 is seen with an up express between Sharnbrook and Oakley in about 1918. (F.W.Goslin)

79.　　Class 2 4-4-0 no.534 heads a down stopping train between Oakley and Sharnbrook. There were black out precautions in WW1 and the engine is fitted with a screen on the tender front to exclude the glare from the fire. (F.W.Goslin)

80.   At Radwell, about midway between Oakley and Sharnbrook, we see an up HST on 11th June 2003. The power car is in Midland Main Line livery followed by red Virgin coaches. The arches of the overbridge present a contrast. That on the left, still showing traces of the orignal red brick, springs from a low level. The 1892 arch of blue Stafford bricks for the goods lines on the right springs at a greater height from vertical sides. This enables it to accommodate the higher goods lines under the same road level. The goods lines between Sharnbrook and a temporary signal box at Milton were brought into use on 25th September 1892. They were extended southwards to Oakley on 9th July 1893, thereby making the goods lines continuous between Bedford and Wellingborough. It was, however, to be another two years before the quadrupling was completed on the London Extension south of Bedford. (G.W.Goslin)

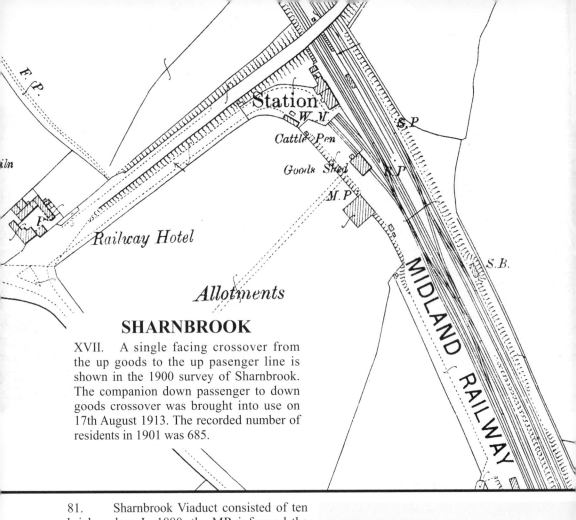

SHARNBROOK

XVII. A single facing crossover from the up goods to the up pasenger line is shown in the 1900 survey of Sharnbrook. The companion down passenger to down goods crossover was brought into use on 17th August 1913. The recorded number of residents in 1901 was 685.

81. Sharnbrook Viaduct consisted of ten brick arches. In 1880, the MR informed the Board of Trade of "Failure in the foundations of one of the piers which has sunk considerably and allowed of several cracks in some of the arches. It has been properly shored up by timber so as to be quite secure". It must have been a great relief to those responsible when the new goods line viaduct was brought into use in March 1880. All traffic was diverted on to the goods lines while a new passenger viaduct was built. We see the old viaduct from the west on 18th March 1881 after it had been taken out of use. Parts of the goods lines viaduct, which was originally built to the same rail level as the passenger viaduct, can be glimpsed behind. After the new passenger viaduct was completed the goods line viaduct was raised to its final level. (British Railways)

82.   We look north from an up train to see the down platform. Access to the up platform was via the road overbridge. In 1903, Sharnbrook had a slip carriage, arriving at 6.3 p.m. off the 5.0 p.m. from St Pancras. The carriage went forward to Irchester and Wellingborough at 6.10 p.m. There were always some calls from passenger trains not stopping at Oakley or Irchester and the station just managed to outlive its neighbours, closing on 2nd May 1960. (Lens of Sutton coll.)

83.　　　Sharnbrook station house is seen in August 1958. The basic design was repeated for the smaller stations throughout from Leicester to Hitchin. Some of the distinctive original window frames have survived on the right. In days when the ethics of hunting for sport were not questioned, special facilities were provided when there was a prospect of additional first class fares. In November 1876, a Notice - Hunting with the Oakley Hounds- gave advice of suitable trains from St Pancras to Bedford and continued - "For the accommodation of hunting gentlemen the train leaving St Pancras at 8.30 a.m. will set passengers down at Sharnbrook or Irchester when the hounds meet in the vicinity of either of these stations." The November1898 WTT included a notice: "During the hunting season special arrangements will be made for the convenience of hunting gentlemen when required. The 10.5 a.m. from St Pancras to Manchester will convey a slip carriage from London to St Albans or Harpenden:, also from Bedford to Sharnbrook or Irchester as may be required of which notice will be given in each case". (Photomatic)

84.　　　Looking south from the road overbridge we see the station in MR days with a down express approaching. Only a small timber shelter was provided on the up platform, although both Oakley and Irchester had more substantial erections. (Lens of Sutton coll.)

85.   No.45137 is on the down goods line with empty coaches and passes the site of Sharnbrook station on 19th May 1980. The ladder junction from down fast to up goods replaced the previous running junctions in 1973, but manual signalling was to last until 17th May 1981, when control of the area finally passed to West Hampstead Power Signal Box. The camera angle is very similar to that of the previous photgraph, taken about 80 years earlier. (K.C.H.Fairey)

86.   In May 2003, St Pancras to Manchester expresses were reinstated due to the WCML upgrading, albeit over a longer route than that previously used. A Virgin liveried "short" HST of six coaches passes the site of Sharnbrook station on 11th June 2003. It had been hired by MML. (G.W.Goslin)

———————▶

88.　　　On 4th February 1909, the Sharnbrook signalman shunted the 2.55am goods train from Bedford to Birmingham from the down goods to the up passenger line. He intended it to continue on the down passenger line but omitted to pull lever no.8 for the crossover. Without ground signals which might have made the signalman aware of his mistake, the train commenced to go forward on the wrong line. When the driver realised the error he only had time to set back to the starting signal and jump clear. The 10.5 pm up express goods from Manchester collided at speed with the Bedford train resulting in the deaths of both driver and fireman. The much damaged locomotive of the train from Manchester is seen after recovery from the wreckage. (G.W.Goslin coll.)

87.　　　EWS no.60045 takes the single goods line at Sharnbrook with a train of empty roadstone wagons on 11th June 2003. The requirements of USA forces in 1943 resulted in the construction of additional sidings on the up side. (G.W.Goslin)

———————▶

89.　　　The engine of the Birmingham goods train was buried in wreckage. Here only the dome is visible. (G.W.Goslin coll.)

NORTH OF SHARNBROOK

90.   Souldrop signal box was photographed on 20th June 1953. The goods lines are out of sight in a deep cutting. The box was closed on 20th December 1966, leaving a long section over the summit from Sharnbrook to Irchester South. (N.D.Mundy)

91.   Compound 4-4-0 no.41083 passes Souldrop box with a short up express on 14th August 1952. (Gresley Society)

92.   Jubilee no. 45561 *Saskatchewan*, with a St Pancras to Sheffield express, is recovering on the 1 in 119 gradient up from a signal check at Souldrop box. (K.C.H.Fairey)

93.   An up coal train was photographed from Souldrop box as it ran down the bank towards Sharnbrook on 7th August 1953. The difference in the levels of the passenger and goods lines is evident. In the distance a haze of steam and smoke drifts from the mouth of Sharnbrook Tunnel. (E.R.Morten)

94.   The 3½ mile Wymington Deviation was opened on 4th May 1884 taking the goods lines through Sharnbrook Tunnel, 1 mile 100 yds long . It gave up coal trains a maximum gradient of 1 in 200 instead of the original three mile climb at 1 in 120 which took the passenger lines over Sharnbrook summit. Class 8F 2-8-0 no.48687 is leaving the tunnel with a coal train on 2nd November 1965. The capacity of the goods lines was cut severely by their reduction to single track between Sharnbrook and Wellingborough in 1987. With geographical correctness, but an unfortunate disregard of tradition, Network Rail refers to the singled bore as Wymington Tunnel. (K.C.H.Fairey)

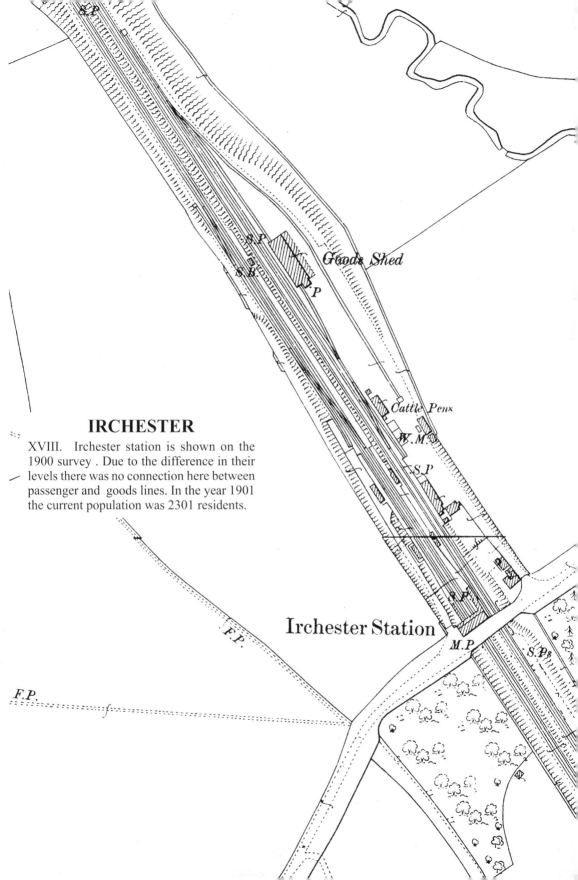

IRCHESTER

XVIII. Irchester station is shown on the 1900 survey . Due to the difference in their levels there was no connection here between passenger and goods lines. In the year 1901 the current population was 2301 residents.

Goods Shed

Cattle Pens

W.M.

Irchester Station

F.P.

F.P.

M.P.

S.P.

95.   Irchester South box is seen looking north in September 1975. It marked the northern end of the Wymington Deviation of the goods lines. Its running junction between passenger and goods lines was taken out of use on 12th October 1969, but the box remained as a block post until 5th December 1987, latterly acting as the fringe box to West Hampstead Power Signal Box. The site now marks the boundary between the areas controlled by West Hampstead and Leicester PSBs. (A. Vaughan)

96.   The half timbered Neo-Tudor main building at Irchester was situated on the road overbridge astride the passenger lines. Irchester lost a large proportion of its passenger business to Rushden when the Higham Ferrers branch was opened, the number of passengers booked falling from 61,896 in 1893 to 25,812 in 1903. (LGRP)

97.　　　With the main building on the overbridge, the platforms were each provided with two sets of shelters, timber at the south end and brick at the north. We look from the end of the up platform to see the structures on the down side. Closure to passengers took place on 6th March 1960. (London Midland Region)

98. Nottingham based class 5 4-6-0 no.44918 passes the box and goods shed with an up express about 1952. (G.W.Goslin)

99. Class 8F 2-8-0 no.8009 passes Irchester on the up goods line with a coal train. The passenger lines can be seen at a lower level on the right. (Gresley Society)

100.   Irchester Junction box is seen in September 1968. It was situated on the east side of the lines in a pole infested photographic location. It was opened on 3rd July 1893 and closed with the Higham Ferrers branch on 21st December 1969. (G.W.Goslin)

Higham Ferrers Branch
RUSHDEN

XIX.   Rushden station is shown six years
after its opening in 1894. There was an
extensive goods yard with a loop from the
single line, controlled by ground frames, but
no provision for crossing trains, the tablet
section being from Irchester Junction to
Higham Ferrers. There was a steady increase
in the number of residents between 1901 and
1961, starting at 12,453 rising to 17,540.

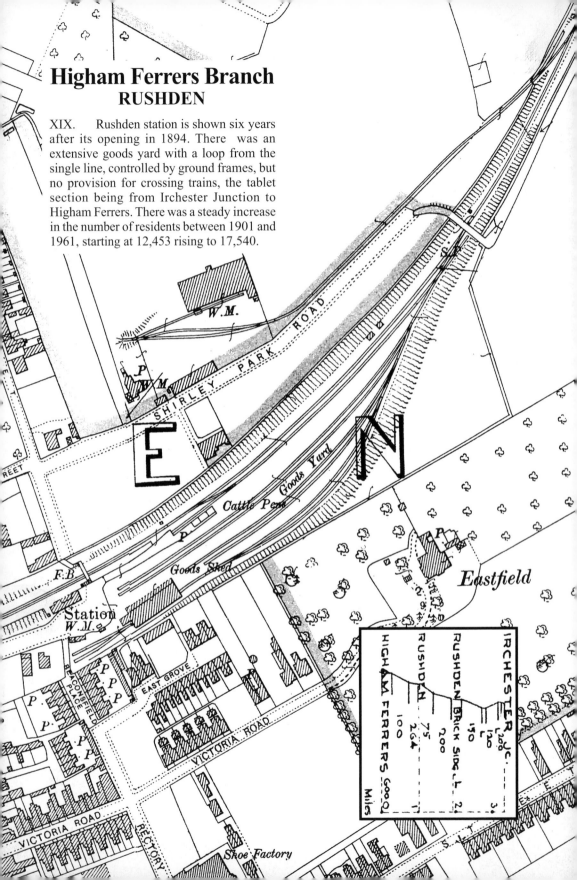

101.   A Saturdays-only through train from Higham Ferrers to Leicester was provided for shoppers in the 1950s. Compound 4-4-0 no.41095 is seen between Irchester Junction and Rushden taking the empty stock to Higham Ferrers for the working on 6th August 1956. (G.W.Goslin)

102.   Rushden station is seen in pre-grouping days with a train entering from Higham Ferrers. Land was available for the provision of a passing loop and a down platform, but the line remained single throughout its life. (Lens of Sutton coll.)

103.   Standard class 2-6-2T no.84006 calls with the branch train to Higham Ferrers on 28th May 1959. Rushden was booking over 100,000 passengers each year up to 1913 but the total had fallen to 75,357 by 1922 probably due to road competition. (K.C.H.Fairey)

FOOTBALL MATCH AT WELLINGBORO',

(Wellingboro' v. Rushden.)

RETURN TICKETS at a fare of 9d. (third class) may be issued to WELLINGBORO' from KETTERING by 2.10 p.m. train, available for returning on the day of issue only.

Pleasure party tickets must be issued, and an account of the bookings furnished to this office.

No. 36.   RUSHDEN TO WELLINGBORO'.   (Additional Train.)

(Football Match at Wellingboro'.)

HIGHAM FERRERS (Empty)..	dep.	1 50 p.m			Empty.	
RUSHDEN .... "	arr.	1 55 ..	WELLINGBORO'	....	dep. 1 20	p.m.
Do.	dep.	2 0 ..	IRCHESTER JUNCTION	....	.. 1 25	..
IRCHESTER JUNCTION	..	2 6 ..	HIGHAM FERRERS	....	arr. 1 35	..
WELLINGBORO'	arr.	2 10 ..				

Mr. Turner to arrange.

A return to be sent me from Rushden, giving detailed particulars of the passengers booked and amount received, by this train.

8th November 1897

HIGHAM FERRERS

XX.   As authorised, the branch was to extend to Raunds but the final portion was not constructed. The layout at Higham Ferrers with the goods shed and signal box to the north of the station was based on that intention and is shown on the 1900 survey. The total number of residents was 2540 in 1901 having risen to 3850 by 1961.

104.   Small boy and driver re-create a famous Southern Railway poster at Higham Ferrers on 2nd October 1954. 0-4-4T no.58091 is about to propel its train to Wellingborough. Such motor train workings on the branch commenced in 1931. (K.C.H.Fairey)

105.   Ex-LYR 2-4-2T no.50650 was at Higham Ferrers on 6th August 1956. Driver W T Fairey is on the platform and Fireman Sam Abbot in the cab. The class had a high reputation in its native area. Shortage of push-pull fitted engines led to the transfer south of 50650 to Wellingborough and 50646 to Bedford.The latter, in particular, was in run down condition and did little active work. (K.C.H.Fairey)

106.   Standard 2-6-2T no. 84007 heads a train for Wellingborough on the last day of passenger services, 13th June 1959. (L.Hanson)

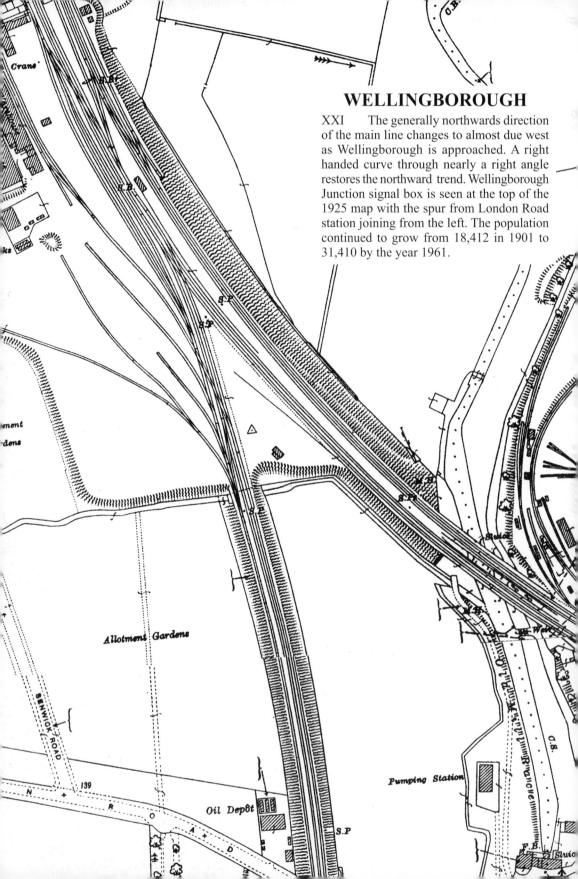

WELLINGBOROUGH

XXI   The generally northwards direction of the main line changes to almost due west as Wellingborough is approached. A right handed curve through nearly a right angle restores the northward trend. Wellingborough Junction signal box is seen at the top of the 1925 map with the spur from London Road station joining from the left. The population continued to grow from 18,412 in 1901 to 31,410 by the year 1961.

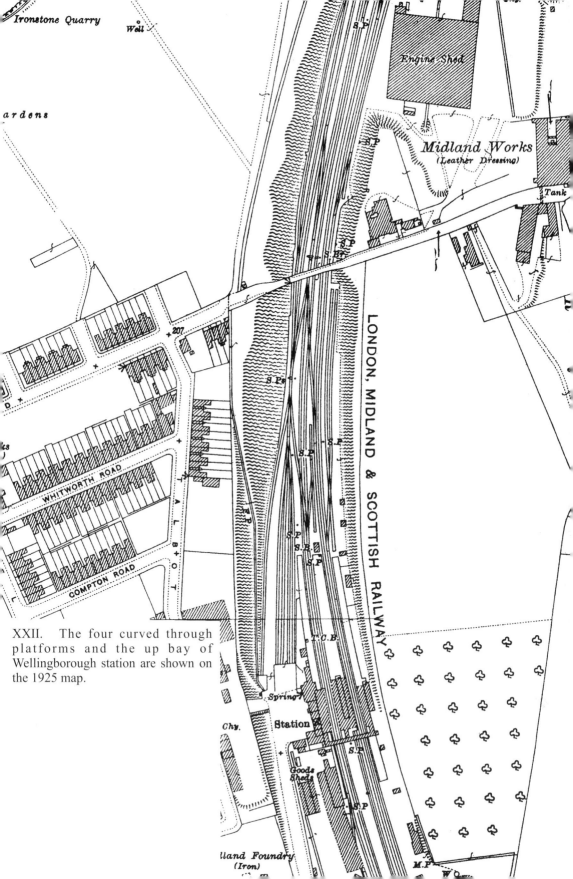

Ironstone Quarry

Well

ardens

Engine Shed

Midland Works
(Leather Dressing)

Tank

S.P.

S.P.

S.P.

T.C.B.

S.Ps.

LONDON, MIDLAND & SCOTTISH RAILWAY

S.P.

S.P.

S.P.

S.B.

S.P.

207

WHITWORTH ROAD

ALBION

COMPTON ROAD

XXII. The four curved through
platforms and the up bay of
Wellingborough station are shown on
the 1925 map.

T.C.B.

Spring

Chy.

Station

Goods
Sheds

S.P.

S.P.

lland Foundry
(Iron)

M.P.

W

107.   Passenger traffic on the branch to Higham Ferrers at times warranted the use only of a single push-pull carriage. 0-4-4T no.58053 propels its train towards Wellingborough on 17th July 1950. (L.Hanson)

108.   At the end of the 1950s, Wellingborough motive power depot undertook some periodic examinations of ex-LNER engines. This resulted in some unexpected types making their trial trips on the Higham Ferrers goods turn. We see class O4/8 no.63472 approaching Wellingborough on 27th May 1959. (K.C.H.Fairey)

109.   A spur ran from Wellingborough Junction, just south of Wellingborough station, to Midland Junction, adjacent to the ex-LNWR Wellingborough London Road station on the Northampton to Peterborough line. Garratt no.47969 crosses the Nene bringing iron ore for Cargo Fleet from Wellingborough London Road Junction to the Midland main line on 27th June 1957. (K.C.H.Fairey)

110.   Passenger services on the spur were withdrawn on 2nd May 1964. Class 2MT 2-6-2T no.41225 is seen at the same location on the last day of working with the 14.30 from Northampton Castle to Kettering. (J.A.Powell)

111.   Among the less usual classes of engine seen on the Higham Ferrers trains was a parallel boiler 2-6-2T, no.40061, photographed when about to leave on 29th June 1957. (K.C.H.Fairey)

112.   Looking north from the up fast platform, we see, on the extreme right, the buffer stops for the bay, which was usually used for departures to Northampton. The up and down slow line platforms were used by the Higham Ferrers trains. (Lens of Sutton coll.)

113.   We look from the north end of the down fast platform to obtain a general view of the station. The curvature is noticeable and there was a limit of 60 mph on the fast lines at Wellingborough although this was actually defined as applying just south of the station, at the junction with the spur to the Northampton line. (Lens of Sutton coll.)

114.　　On 2nd September 1898, a St Pancras to Manchester express travelling at high speed was derailed by a luggage barrow which had rolled off the down platform at Wellingborough. There was much destruction of the timber bodied carriages and twelve lives were lost. It was suspected that some boys had tampered with the barrow but this was never proved. (G.W.Goslin coll.)

115.　　A three-car articulated diesel set ran experimentally from Bedford in 1939. It was tried on the Bletchley/Cambridge line and was then used on workings from Bedford to Nottingham and St Pancras. This promising development was cut short by the outbreak of WWII. The unit is seen in the down platform at Wellingborough. (Real Photographs)

116.   The provision of a temporary footbridge made possible this unusual view of no.45148 entering the up platform station near the Station signal box on 2nd April 1983. The box was to last over four years after the photograph was taken, being closed on 5th December 1987. (K.C.H.Fairey)

117.   No.45135 brings a coal train through the then derelict up slow platform on 12th September 1974. (K.C.H.Fairey)

118.   No.45135 leaves the station with a down express on 4th April 1983. Except for the odd relief, responsibilty for all such workings passed to HSTs in the following month. (K.C.H.Fairey)

119.   Power Car no.43052 is the leading vehicle of an up HST seen about to depart on 11th February 1988. (K.C.H Fairey)

120.   Two-car class 170 unit no.110 is in the up platform on a trial run on 1st April 1999, prior to the commencement of services on 30th May. Seventeen two-car sets were provided initially but the standard class capacity of 97 seats predictably proved to be inadequate. After a short time in service additional non-driving coaches had to be ordered to make up three car sets. (K.C.H.Fairey)

MP Middleton Press

Easebourne Lane, Midhurst, W Sussex. GU29 9AZ Tel: 01730 813169 Fax: 01730 812601
Email: sales@middletonpress.co.uk   www.middletonpress.co.uk
If books are not available from your local transport stockist, order direct post free UK.